Poems

POEMS

BY R. C. PHILLIMORE
WITH AN INTRODUCTION
BY JOHN MASEFIELD

By the grace of God I took
From my lady's hands this book,
And herein for my lady's sake
Her songs I'll make.

LONDON : SIDGWICK & JACKSON, LTD.
3, ADAM STREET, W.C.   MCMXIII

INTRODUCTION

Mr. Phillimore's poems have a quality that
is as rare in literature as in other things—the
quality of personality or individual point of
view. Men's minds, whatever their variety of
type, are seldom so variously active as to be
distinct in texture. Their activities tend to be
confined within conventional limits, which,
though they may suit the type, or even the race,
are cramping to the person. It is only when
the person or individual emerges, however
imperfectly, from the clogging level of what is
commonly thought or usually done, that the
attention is aroused, the imagination set free,
and a new thing added to the mind. Writers,
as a class, are as subject to convention as their
fellows; none but the great are free, none but
the free are great. But every mark of freedom
is a sign of greatness, and Mr. Phillimore at once

makes this claim upon us—that he is not one of those who are poets as they would be tallow chandlers, merely from some fondness for smoothness, but because he has the strength to be personally alone, uttering things after his own fashion, stamped with his own mark, asking nothing more " than to enjoy Delight with Liberty," by being himself and uttering himself. This is the rare thing in a literary age when writers are book-sodden, and this quality Mr. Phillimore has. Whether one likes or dislikes what he writes, one is conscious that it comes from the full strength of a personality, with a man's nature behind it.

Many poets win honour with poems which express only a part, or a single desire, of their natures. In Mr. Phillimore's lyrics one feels that the writer has been ordering to gentle measures not one but many sides of himself, many interests and delights in kinds of life both interesting and delightful, so that none of his nature might be without its music. This keeping of balance and order in vital interests, allowing none to warp the nature, but exercising all, gives health and strength to a man and power to a poet. Those who fit up one room with all their treasures may delight a gaudy mood, but the more chosen habitation is that mansion of the mind where many chambers are lit, swept, and habitable.

Mr. Phillimore's variety of subject makes his work companionable to many moods; and it is by considering his subjects that we can best come to a knowledge of his poetical place. Frequently a line or couplet will indicate a poet's nature as completely as a volume, and it seems to us that the living quality of Mr. Phillimore's interests is perfectly displayed in the merry poem " To All Land Children," in the lines—

" I would rather play with a conger eel,
 If only because such a beast can feel
 When I pinch his tail, than with all the flowers
 That do nothing but grow through the livelong hours."

Something alive that can act and be handled gives a flavour of life to thought, and, as Mr. Phillimore says,
" Gives just the fun
That makes a charming companion."

INTRODUCTION

Continually throughout the book the reader
finds this happiness in having life to handle
made the *motif* of poem or image, as in the fine
poem beginning:

" Would you go out into the void place of death ?"

and more certainly and completely in the opening stanza of the eighth poem, where the philos-
ophy of a life has been wittily pressed into five
lines.   With this sense of the happiness of pos-
sessing life there is a powerful sense of the moral
use of life, in continual just endeavour towards
men and work (expressed well in " The House of
Flint " and boldly in the poem " Content "), and
also that rebellious sense which has cried
" Escape !" in our literature, in this or that
direction, for nearly a century, to show that
the world's endeavour towards men and work
at the present time has failed both in achieve-
ment and in aim.

The ideal is man's hope transfigured, and in
the minds of poets it is often made the brighter
by the feeling that it has gone from the world
in some gradual fading of the soul.   We all have
glimpses of some illuminated time now gone:

INTRODUCTION

to Mr. Phillimore these glimpses come in poign-
ant moments, when the swiftness or passion
of some movement of London work-girls flinging
bread to the gulls, or the fall of music played by
gipsies in the wilds, suggests a grace or fire now
crushed or gone from life. Other poems show
him conscious of a time when there was stricter
justice between master and man, and a stricter
exaction of fine work, but in these poems he
writes of that earlier time, suspected by scien-
tists, but told of by the poets, when the individual was fine and ecstasy was daily bread,
and the possession of that bread not, as now,
a passport out of civilization, but the knowledge
of the heart of life. The gipsy poems have all
the charm that gipsying has for us; they give
us that sense of the desire to escape which is
often like a drunkenness upon the city dweller,
and they are full of that respect (it is very
nearly envy) which all the civilized feel for
men and women who have been strong enough
to give up everything in order to possess their
own souls, facing the wilderness proudly with
a little music and a tale or two.

INTRODUCTION

Of the other sides of Mr. Phillimore's work, one other may be noticed here: his interesting metrical retelling of some of the Arthurian story. Against the Arthurian story it may be objected that Malory has told it finally in a fitting form, and that since we have it in prose we should therewith be content. Similar objections were raised, no doubt, when Shakespeare made free with Holinshed. The two or three great English stories should be a quarrying ground for the imaginations of our poets, and Mr. Phillimore's " Betraying of Guinever," though too much a paraphrase and too little a plucking out of the passionate soul, has a dignity and power. It is more an opening than a completed poem, for being too much of a paraphrase it suffers from Malory's formlessness, but its suggestion and force of narrative make one hope that Mr. Phillimore will do more poems like it.

There are other gay and gentle poems which deserve mention, particularly those two or three which show a sensitive understanding of the imagination of the child. If Mr. Phillimore

INTRODUCTION

has failed in this or that point, in the turning of
a line or the tagging of a stanza, his work has
a rightness of thought and feeling which is
always there and always charming; and since,
in a literary age, most people can do mere
writing, we will turn to him for what is living
and human, and to his critics for the rest.

JOHN MASEFIELD.

June 10, 1913.

CONTENTS

CONTENTS

1. THE BOY'S LAMENT

I WOULD no birds were singing,
I would no plants could grow,
I would that everything did wear
A solemn dress of woe.

For, ah is me ! my love is dead,
My love is dead,
And it makes me sorrow so.

They say that my love was lovely,
They say that my love was fair :
" Her face was like a picture,
And the bonniest nut-brown hair."

But she was just my love to me,
My love to me;
For nothing else do I care.

Oh ! I would I could go to my true love,
Just once her face to see ;
For I know that nothing can make me glad,
Can make me glad,
But her sweet company.

And I cannot believe that my love,
My own true love,
Would be sorry of me.

2. TO ALL LAND CHILDREN

Come, dear children, come and play
In the purple pools by the edge of the bay,
Where the rocks are green and the seaweed red,
And the hermit crab lies late a-bed.

Oh ! why do you play with the garden flowers
That fade when they're picked in a few short
        hours ?
Oh ! why make a pet of a dull land rose
That thinks stupid thoughts that nobody knows ?

When here in this pool in the slippery rocks,
By untying the sea-wrack's knotty locks,
You can see strange orange snails crawl by,
And him that has the scarlet dye:

See fishes dart in the depths below,
Old, gouty limpets walking slow,
And the barnacles, that open their bony eyes
To squint at the crimson anemonies.

One day, when the tide is frightfully low,
Out to the edge of the bay we'll go,
To look at the roses of the seas,
The monster crassicornisses.

He cares not to grow in a garden prim,
No gardener man looks after him,
But neatly and well like a dandy he's dressed
In a coat of frieze and a scarlet vest.

And as to his thoughts, they are plain to see,
For he makes no manner of mystery,
But with long arms waving far and wide,
Seeks for his tea at the turn of the tide.

Unless he be cursed with a priggish mind,
No child could a better playmate find;
For such innocent manners give just the fun
That makes a charming companion.

I would rather play with a conger-eel,
If only because such a beast can feel
When I pinch his tail, than with all the flowers
That do nothing but grow through the livelong
      hours.

So come, dear children, come and play
With the strange sea-beasts at the edge of the
      bay,
And bring them meat and pieces of bread,
That the hermit crabs may be duly fed.

3. THE OULAD NAIL'S INVITATION

Now that the feast is nearly over,
Come let us leave the glamour of the street !
For the evening has invited
To the courtyard dimly lighted
My unreluctant feet.

When faint from the market of the perfumes
The scent of musk and cinnamon is blown,
By a wind that, incense breathing,
Through the gateway passes, wreathing
Marble and carven stone,

I will bring you to a place where all is quiet,
And spread before your eyes a soft divan,
Made pleasant for your dreaming
With silks of strangest seeming,
And with carpets of Kerouan.

4. FERNHURST

THE little hill falling in steep degrees
Is half made bare, half hid in last year's leaves,
By fitful gusts of summer wind, that weaves
The broken air through scarce interstices.

Here foliage of the many-branchèd trees
Almost across the dim horizon reaches,
And burnished stems of elfin-haunted beeches
Above the slope show their wind-knotted knees.

There, outlined dark, the rolling Sussex weald,
And far-off sky through arches yellow-green,
Depth beyond depth of deepness is revealed—
A shadowy land, seen sunlit boughs between.

So pleasant is the place, that all are fain
Long here to linger, gazing on the plain.

5. THE POET AND HIS MISTRESS

POET.

COME, love, we'll make a bargain !
For half a ream of song
You shall make me one small promise,
To love me my whole life long.

MISTRESS.

When waste and rotten refuse
For gold can bartered be,
Then shall you sell your rubbish
And buy one kiss from me.

6. " I AM ALWAYS ASKING MY FRIENDS WHETHER LIFE IS WORTH LIVING TO THEM "

WOULD you go out into the void place of death
Where is no firelight flicker of a friend,
Nor even a little candle of love to lend
Light to the night, that nightens without end ?

Would you forget the good times you have
    known
That make your present living seem so waste,
Or has not one, not one fair field been sown
In all the weary acreage of the past ?

Or are you fearing that from life's small store,
You've stolen more than what you can repay ?
Know there is piled upon God's granary floor
More than you'll take away.

There were great seasons in the boundless past,
Great frosts, great western winds and wandering
    rain ;
And God has reaped a million crops of grain,
And Man a little tithe thereof has ta'en.

And if sometimes somewhere the store looks
    small,
And if sometimes somewhere the light seems
    dim,
Your thought has failed, the harvest not at all;
Heaped with God's reapings is the world's wide
    rim.

7.

RIGHT glad should I be
To be born in the South,
Were I beast, or man, or tree.
It's a hateful drive
To keep alive
In the bitter North Countree.

8.

I LOVE one self, the small myself I know,
With thinking brain and loving heart, and feet
That wander daily down the solid street:
A whole intent to fashion as it may
Some other whole out of life's supple clay.

The other self I love not—that is God,
Or rather is the elusive infinite,
Of hopes and terrors strangely composite,
That in his own image since the world began
Each man has made anew, crying that God made
    man.

9. THE COLLECTOR'S LOVE SONG

LITTLE sweet flower, 'tis you that are
On the lid of the ginger-jar;
No one else could have such sweet
Delicate hands and painted feet,
Or so contrive to carry your fan
As to melt the might of a metal man.

I wish I were the man who drew
Your features on the crackled blue;
I wish I were the painter too;
I wish, in fact, I could divine
How to limn that lovely line,
Paint it, and burn it, and make it mine—
Make, in fact, the thing called You.

All my life I would repeat
Just those hands and painted feet,
And give you just a yellow fan
As would melt the might of a metal man:
Lest, little flower, you should break
Your porcelain heart for some ruffian's sake.

10. THE HOUSE OF FLINT

HERE is the master mason's mark
And here the humble craftsman's dint,
As clean and clear and sharp as when
They scratched them on you, house of flint !

You have no pointing to decay,
No face of stone to waste away.
They put you here, and here you stay,
In the hollow below the pilgrims' way,
Unchanged, unaltered, hard as flint.

Men do not build your like to-day,
But a great crafty show is made,
Though little the poor craftsman's paid.
The joints fall out, the bricks decay,
The bath-stone lintels waste away:

And the mark of the master-man is set
Where the slipping slates let in the wet,
Where the paper peels from the sweating wall,
And patches of plaster crack and fall.

One day when labouring is fair,
When men and things are made to wear,
When folks would rather pay for care,
Than spend their money in repair—

I will seek out some craftsmen rare,
And somewhere beneath the pilgrims' way,
Where old and branching yews grow grey,
I will dig in the side of the old chalk down,
And burn some lime and knap some flint.

And I'll scratch my master mason's mark
Beside the craftsmen's cunning dint,
On such a house as you were when
Men dared to write their names in flint.

11. THE CITY DUSTHEAPS

It is bitter, bitter cold to-day,
And the ice is out to sea;
Therefore the seagulls are in to-day,
And over the river grim and grey,
And under the granite walls they play—
Play like children and scream and fight,
Not altogether from pure delight,
But watching, perchance, if down the tide
Some part of a fish that once was fried,
Or a tasty bit from a pig's inside,
Or, failing that, some meat or bread
May escape from the plates of the quite well-bred
To where, by God's grace, the poor are fed.

London is a dull grey place,
In winter especially:
Seldom you see a happy face
Anywhere about the place.
Therefore I count it a special grace,
Something unhuman and divine
When I get a beauty of limb or line,
Or a wonderful colour on the town,
As the old boiled sun is settling down
Over outlines blurred and gritty
Where nothing is clean, nor new, nor pretty,
In the waste places of the city.
And if when the seagulls wheel in the air
Over the murky river,
Against the head of the granite stair
I catch a glimpse of red-gold hair,

And a grace of limb that I knew somewhere
In a time that's not now, in a place not here.
And if the seagulls call loud and clear,
I may in the lift of the seagulls' cry
Forget that nations come here to die,
Irish and Jew and Gipsy rai,
And think that such colour and line and limb
Come straight through the ages dull and dim
From off the sun's great flaming rim.
Oh ! it's only the girls from the dustheaps
Where it is squashy underfoot
With cabbages, where broken shards
Stink as they litter up the yards,
Where old love-letters and business cards,
And waste of morals and art and mind,
Compete together in the wind
To make a hell of a special kind.

They have come to forget that they are fed,
Red hair and black, from the refuse shed
In the splendour of throwing the sea-gulls bread.

12.

To us she was a beautiful thing,
Delicate, wise, and strong;
But to him she was just everything,
And he to her did belong.

We thought, that she should have to die
Was cruel and wrong and bad;
But he just took it patiently,
For she was all that he had.

Our minds were racked to find the cause
Why the world went so astray;
But his was set to know the laws
She'd want him to obey.

13. CONTENT

I THANK whatever God there be,
That he has deigned to fashion me,
That he has taken clay so strong,
And washed so well and pugged so long,
And burnt such cruel flames among,
That when he strikes I ring with song.

That when he builds me in his wall
I do not cause the work to fall,
But bear my weight and take my place;
And when, to give me greater grace,
He cuts in me a cunning chase
I do not spoil the bonded face.

If other bricks are made awry,
Then let them in the footings lie,
And not complain;
For should he mould me all again,
A thing so vile that life were pain,
Yet would I live and bring him gain.

14. DISCONTENT

WHEN the dark earth after a storm of rain
Exhales the fragrant gladness of her rest,
The aspen leaves, freed from the strong south-
    west,
And turning to their ancient place again,
With whispering leaves persistently complain,
That they have been by cruel gales oppressed.
Though, now by balmy airs soothed and car-
    ressed,
Ever they make their murmuring disdain.
  So life to me is nothing but a sighing,
" Ah ! love is hard ! Such cruel, bitter pain !"
E'en when I might forget, I still am fain
To murmur on in mournful sonnet strain,
With long-drawn cadence rising, falling, dying,
Mocking old echoes of my passionate crying.

15. A CONFESSION

I USED to think when I was young,
That many were the May-days in the spring,
And that love of life and the life of love
Were the very same thing.

But now that I am old and grey
I do not care so much for May,
And rather sickly the thoughts seem
That made my dream.

I used to think in the beggar's bowl,
In the tramp's long hair,
There struggled unheeded a noble soul
With a fate unfair.

But now that wisdom counts for much,
And money for more,
A little I look down upon
The tired and poor.

And if I pity have to spare
Which I have not often,
I send it labelled " With great care "
The woes to soften
Of those who, like myself, have forced
Their adult souls to hurry after
Knowledge and wealth and power, and lost
Youth and its laughter.

16. SIR BREUSE SANS PITIE

In vain I looked for comforting
To every loved and lovely thing,
To the apple-blossom on the boughs in spring,
To the strange wild songs that thrushes sing:
For last year's joy in me was dead,
And no new joy would come instead.

The apple-blossom on the boughs in spring,
And the strange wild songs that thrushes sing,
Were only to me an endless string
Of colours and sounds without meaning:
I looked in vain for pitying
To every growing, living thing.

For everything answered : " You have no pity,
Pity and love and sweet mercy:
Therefore we say you can never see
Beauty in blossom on bough and tree,
Nor hear the things that the wild birds say,
Though wildly they pipe to you all day.

" You have closed your eyes, that you may not see
The sorrowful flowers that are torn from the tree,
And the cages of birds that are not free:
For ever you lived without pity,
Pity and love and sweet mercy.

" So, till you learn the pitying
Of every dying and wilted thing,
Of the withered bloom in the frosty spring,
Of the poor caged birds that cannot sing,
Of the meanest, legless worms that crawl,
Of the jellies that cannot move at all,

" Your life shall be as a barren spring
Wherein no wanton thrush shall sing,
No fairies play in a mushroom ring,
Nor apples burst into blossoming:
You will look in vain for comforting
To every lovely and loving thing."

17. ON THE LOSS OF MY LADY'S
GREAT HAIR

My lady has shorn her lovely hair,
Ah's me !
She tells me, that I must not care,
Woe's me !
That she has shorn her glossy hair,
Her thick, dark hair.
Ah's me !

She tells me, that true love is blind,
And spurns the form and seeks the mind.
But woe is me !
She was unkind
To cut and maim her flowing hair.

I look for it; it is not there,
Ah's me !
'Tis a bitter grief, and I must care,
Woe's me !
For I loved the length of her lovely hair,
And I worshipped God who put it there.
Ah's me !

But there is no worship now for me,
I see no beauty in bird or tree ;
For birds have feathers, and trees have leaves
And, ah, woe's me !
But my sad heart grieves
For the passionate coils of my lady's hair.

18. THE EPIC OF PEAT

A THOUSAND bards have sung of the harvest of
    golden grain,
And hundreds of the harvestless sea,
But of the peat not one.

And the man who tells the measure of what the
    season has borne,
A couple more acres of pasture
For an acre less of corn,

Has again and again forgotten to make his tale
    complete,
By measuring on the bare mountain
The acreage of the peat.

For a million years it has grown there on miles
    and miles of moor,
Where the little people sowed it
For the harvesting of the poor.

The crops that are of men's sowing have need
    of the sun and the rain,
That there may be plenty at haytime,
And a glory of golden grain.

But those that planted the bogland take no care
    for the bare hillside,
Yet always the brown of the mountain
Turns purple at harvest-tide.

Yet think not they willed that by mortals the
    crop should be easily earned;
For before in the cradle they're fitted
Three times must the peat sods be turned.

And the man that in windy April to the cutting
    will not go,
They have sworn, that in bleak December
He shall reap but frost and snow.

So he who is warned goes early to cut the long,
    thin vein,
And mark on the purple pavement
The slanting teeth of his slane.

Next, if he follows the custom, in sixes his
    turves he will stand;
But afterwards in dozens
On the driest spittle of land.

And last, when the summer is waning and the
    glorious autumn weather
Has ripened the lazy barley
And painted the crimson heather,

He will empty his brimming basket, that close
    to the cabin door,
On high the sloping peat-stack
May rise from the reedy floor.

19. TO THE CUSHENDUN CORNCRAKE

Pardon me, bird, if I did you a wrong,
If I cursed you over loud or long !
Pardon, if your lovely song
Seemed to me a little long.
In fact, if I longed to do you a wrong,
Even perchance your neck to break
For making such a hateful scrake,
Saying : " Crake, crake, crake,
Is my love awake ?"
Till your sweet love answered you out of the
      brake :
" Crake, crake, crake,
My heart is awake,
And watches ever for my true love's sake !"

To-night you are a memory,
A sweet voice heard across the sea,
Calling, calling, calling me
From wheresoever I chance to be
To follow you over the misty sea,
To follow, to follow, to follow and take
The road that winds by the misty lake
To where my true love lies awake,
A little sad for her true love's sake,
And a little because from out of the brake
Your voices make
Such a hateful crake
That the devil himself would be kept awake.

20. TO DARWIN, HUXLEY, TYNDALL, RUSKIN, MORRIS, CLOUGH

ELDER men who, unafraid,
Thought and said,
Wrought and made
Fabrics that can never fade,
Fashions young
In sunlight flung
On a world in shade.

Masters from whom men to-day
Turn away
To think and say
Words ye rejected yesterday,
And nothing create
New or great,
But to the old gods pray.

Say, when to-morrow comes, shall we
Bow the knee
To what they see;
Or shall we arise and fight as ye,
The old moulds breaking
And new moulds making
In the smithy of the to be ?

21. OCTOBER

There's a wonderful wind in the trees to-day,
It makes my spirit light and gay;
For it tells of the things that the thin clouds say
When they go galloping together.

22. PEA-PICKING

In the pine country where, by the water,
There is a place that from villas is free,
On the heath hillocks, close to the roadside,
Still pitched are the grey tents of Eli Lee.

Of late this choice neighbourhood much has
      developed,
Lost is the glory of heather and tree;
Ten years of red-brick civilization
Have narrowed the circle round Eli Lee.

Most of the thousands that dwell in the pine-
      lands
Are wealthy and stodgy and nothing to me,
But I'm friends with the son of a Jew auc-
      tioneer,
And, perhaps, with the daughter of Eli Lee.

He is a gentleman of good education,
And a musical taste from his Jew pedigree
Of which he's not proud, but of his position,
So far from the squalour of Eli Lee.

She stands aloof from the race that has con-
      quered
The world, in her pride of a Roman rani;
No Gorgiko blood has defiled the crati,
Kali's the tsarvi of Eli Lee.

In the pine-country the selling of villas
Is as paying to Jews as most business must be;
But I fear the pea harvest that falls to her reaping
Scarce enriches the daughter of Eli Lee.

And we of the race of world-conquering mongrels
Bow down to the Jew whom our master we see,
In cheaply producing that civilization
Which purges waste products like Eli Lee.

Small matter to us that the rai we've rejected
Has a far-away look in its eyes, that's the key
To the things that the West has forgot of its
    childhood !
We've no care for the wasting of Eli Lee.

So, though we grow women as fair as the morn-
    ing,
And poets in plenty to extoll their degree,
It seems we must kill just that type which is
    Beauty,
And the song-soul of race of Eli Lee.

23. HUNGARIAN MUSIC

Give me one more Tśardaś,
One more chance to wander away
To the level lands where wandering was better
Than in this barren wilderness to-day.

I have forgotten, Gipsy player, I have forgotten
So many things I learnt when I was young;
But more than all the things that I've forgotten
Your taćo romani gillis to-day have sung.

They have told me of the far-off Eastern
        countries
Where unstolen cherries drop from off the tree;
And brought me to the taćo romani homeland,
Where the taćo romani tśals lived free.

Apre o drum, apre o drum !
'Tis a sun-loved land whence your music has
        come:
A land which the free wind sweeps with the
        odour
Of heather and gorse in bloom:

A great waste land with open spaces
Where your children played, and romani graces
Were seen in the beauty of your sweet tśais'
        faces,
The sun-loved land whence your music has
        come.

And wisdom that not even the rai has dreamed
        of,
And knowledge that the race has never known,
And all that might have been if only,
For me from that land have come.

I have forgotten Gipsy player, I have forgotten
So many things I'd try to learn again,
If only you would give me one more Tśardaś:
Servus, Viva, Eljen !

24. IN A BY-STREET AT FOGARAŚ

Into that silence where our brother is
Can come no noisy music.   He lies still:
So still, that all the neighbours call him dead.
Only his wife, fanning his white tired face,
Thinks he may hear her voice.   Unceasingly
She cries his spirit back, bidding him remember
How well she loved him, bidding him forget,
That she had ever spoken one harsh word,
Or done one thing amiss to vex his soul.

Inside the low, dark-ceilinged, hot-packed room,
Amidst the neighbours crowded, listening,
Watching and weeping, the house-master lies
    still.
Outside are we, his friends, his Tzigan brothers,
Playing in sadness the soft, bitter music
That he, a Tzigan, played when a Tzigan lay
    dead.

25. THE BETRAYING OF GUINEVER

AND therewithal there came an angry voice
Above the noise of the unstilled, wandering wind,
" Traitor knight, traitor knight, Sir Launcelot
    du Lake,
Come out of the Queen's chamber !"
Then Sir Launcelot looked to see what armour
    hung
On the walls of that fair chamber, that withal
Lightly he might be dressed for knightly deeds.
But " Alas !" cried out Queen Guinever, " I
    have
None armour, though in mercy there is sore need,
For by their noise I hear the noble knights
Have come in a great host and surely armed.
Wherefore I dread now is our long love ended,
That hath endured through many a summer's
    maying
And many a winter's cold." But ever in one
Sir Mordred and Sir Agravaine cried out:
" Traitor knight, come out of the Queen's
    chamber !"
Then shouted out Sir Launcelot, and said:
" Oh mercy ! I may not bear this shameful
    noise."
So he took his lady, the Queen, in his arms and
Kissed her, and said: " Most noble, Christian
    Queen,
As you have ever been my special lady,
And I at all times been your true, poor knight,
For whose sweet sake in many jousts and battles
Much worship have I won, and never yet

Failed you in right or wrong, now I beseech,
That you will pray for my soul, if here I'm
    slain."
And, as he finished, louder came the noise;
For the knights had got a great form from the
    hall,
And therewithal they rushed against the door.
Then Launcelot was fain to see those men,
And bade them leave their rushing while he
    drew
The bolt along the stancheon. So when the
    door was free,
He held it with his left hand, not too wide,
Till anon and anon came striding in a knight,
Sir Colerevance of Gore, and with his sword
Struck one great blow; but Launcelot put that by
And gave him such a buffet on the helm,
That grovelling dead he fell within the chamber.
Then Launcelot shut the mightily clanging door
Against that press of knights, and Guinever
Came nigh to where the dead man lay, and put
Lightly his armour upon Launcelot.
But ever Sir Mordred and Sir Agravaine,
Above the noise of the wild wandering wind
That made great dole about the corridor,
Cried out: " Traitor knight, traitor knight, Sir
    Launcelot,
Come out of the Queen's chamber !" and again:
" Fie on thee, traitor ! Maugre thy head, thou
    diest !"
But Sir Launcelot's anger swelled as a great sea :
So, as they thrust, he let the door fall wide,
And mightily and knightly he strode out
Amongst them all: and none of all those knights

Could stand against the buffets that he gave.
And so, tracing and traversing, here and there,
He laid full fourteen knights cold to the earth,
All but Sir Mordred, who stirred up this strife,
Being wood mad with malice toward the Queen;
And he was sore wounded, so he fled with dole.
Then somewhat wearily Sir Launcelot turned
    back,
And looked and saw, that Guinever had swooned.
But anon it came to pass, that she might speak,
And call unto him softly: " Marvel not,
That I should make this fare; for wit ye well
Now is all true love brought unto an end
Which had a splendid springtide, ere King Mark
Traitorously slew Tristram and Belle Isolt.
To-night on me is the burden that she bore,
To-night with Isolt linked we are in blame.
' Tell Guinever,' she said, ' I send her word,
There are four lovers only in this land—
That is, Queen Guinever and Launcelot,
Tristram de Liones and Queen Isolt.'
For now a greater man than was King Mark,
Arthur to wit, will ever be our foe,
Who, though a noble King, is without mercy
Where that he deems his honour is at fault:
And cruel is the law unto true lovers,
And by the law I must be judged to death."
Then Launcelot cried unto her: " Guinever !"
And again he cried: " My first love and my last,
Come with me now, and ever will I prove
Upon the bodies of all perilous knights
The truth of mine own lady and her love."
" Nay !" said Queen Guinever, and again : " Not
    so !

For thus should we break up the Table Round,
The which fair fellowship was first ordained
In token of the roundness of the world,
That every worshipful knight might there
    repair
To right the evil customs of the time:
And especially that never damosel
By any dangerous deed should be betrayed,
But holpen in her quest. And of them all
Ye have the praise to be the noblest knight:
Nor came there maid, nor damosel distressed
To cry on Launcelot, but ye alway
Upon you took her quarrel without stint.
Yet wit I well no lady was beloved
Of Launcelot, but all only Queen Guinever.
And for the sake of that I will our love
Shall be a token alway to true knights;
Therefore am I so careful of this blame,
That through us twain perished love's fellowship
And the good customs of the Table Round."

But so she said no more; for the day brake,
And the loud wind went before it, making dole.

26. THE POET CANNOT STAY IN
THE SOUTH COUNTRY

I WANT to be singing of apple-trees
That grow in a garden fair,
And of birds that chirp in the balmy breeze
That whispers there.

But somehow my song is away with me,
And takes me down to the songless sea
Where the wandering winds with a howling rout
Roar whirling words in a wordless shout.

I want to love my sweetheart dear,
My helpmate true,
And do throughout the livelong year
What we planned to do.

But somehow my heart is away with me,
And takes me down to the shiftless sea,
Bidding me never to rest till I find
Some fairer love that is more to my mind.

I want to cease such imagining
Which is utterly vain,
And try to make a musical thing
In a measured strain.

But somehow my soul is away from me,
And longs to be lost in the soulless sea
Where there is neither right nor wrong,
But mermen's dance and mermaids' song.

27. QUESTION AND ANSWER

" WHEN the winds that love her
Turn the Spring to woo,
What are you to me, love ?
What am I to you ?

" When the birds are pairing
Merrily in the tree,
What am I to you, love ?
What are you to me ?

" When the grass i' the morning
Is kissed by the frosty dew,
What am I to you, love ?
What are you to me ?

" When the waves lie quiet,
And still is the sea,
What am I to you, love ?
What are you to me ?"

" Ah ! if you would only
Deign to tell me true
Just that little secret,
What I am to you,

" Then, oh dearest lover,
I would just make free
To tell you very plainly
What you are to me."

28. DUNWICH

The Child.

" I cannot love you, sullen sea, that will not
    play,
But blubber on the pebbly beach the whole dull
    day.
You ought to have tremendous tides to drive
    your waves away,
Out, out, ever so far, to the outside edge of the
    bay.
That a child might tread, tread, tread, and
    dance
On the red, ribbed sand;
And wisely, wisely watch askance,
Lest, perchance,
Such a flat, flat fish advance
With flapping tail, to join the dance
On the red, ribbed sand."

The Sea.

" I have no time with a child to play, on the
    red, ribbed sand:
For busily I do the will of the winds to waste
    this land.
They bade me with my sweeping share plough
    out the unfurrowed strand
And undermine the tumbling town, that its
    footings might not stand.
I make it crack, crack and fall
Into my sea.

And pride of ancient chartered wall,
And church towers tall,
Rich merchants' mansions, the great guildhall,
And the craftsman's cot—'tis the same for all
In my sullen sea."

29. INNISFREE

My mistress walked along the shore,
The shore of Innisfree,
And her voice, that is as the soft west wind,
Kept calling, calling me.

" Come follow, come follow, come follow," she
    said,
" Wherever my bare brown feet can tread
On kelp, or on rock, or in the pool in the hollow,
There you must follow, must follow, must follow,
If lover of mine you would be."

But I was afraid of the angry sea
And the white waves' fleck,
And I feared to tread on the slippery rock
And the red sea wrack.

" Who fears to follow, to follow," said she,
" I fear that never my lover shall be."
And she laughed at my sorrow, and scorned me
    to follow
Where the wild spray lept from the chafing
    hollow
And beat on her face and neck.

30. THE POET RECEIVETH SMALL COMFORT FROM HOLY MATRIMONY

How sweet it is, that by one's side
One has a wife both true and tried
To whom with just the right confusion
One can repeat one's last effusion !
Say, that with burning of much oil
In midnight lamps, from torturing toil
And hard abstraction,
One feels one has obtained a whole
Not altogether perfect, still
A product of the working will,
The sensitive soul and some poor skill,
A chose in action.
And then, her mercy humbly praying,
One dares to seek her judgment, laying
One's soul before her eyes, resigned
If some rare beauties faults she'll find,
Think this line halting, that thought blind.
Of course she's right, but never mind.
What does she say ?   Be quick !   Be kind !
I wait.   And sudden comes " Ha hah !"

Alas ! the same with my impromptu,
A trilling, thrilling thing that haunts you:
From tunes of birds and summer rain
Built up and bound with pity and pain.
I warble it in her ears.   Again
Breaks in that damning old refrain,

" Ha hah !   Ha hah !"
Perhaps it is her mind is gay,
In merry meads her fancies play
With elfish friends in the new-mown hay,
Making it lighter.
So I devise a funny jest
From Chesterton and Shaw compressed
With something added of the best
In last week's comic paper.
I smile and hand her this.   Am sure
At the sixth line she'll say " Ha hah !"
I wait.   There's silence.
Her great eyes
Have loosed the starlight of the skies
And dully fix them on the floor.
I wait.   At last she kind of sighs :
" I've told you many times before
Your Saxon wit is just a bore :
I'll burn it if there's one word more."

And yet she says she'd have me write !
Good God ! am I demented quite ?

31. INVOCATION TO MILTON

Oh, thou whose unlighted eyes
Looked on God in Paradise,
Who felt on sin, at sin's beginning,
Flame the sword, that scorched the sinning,
In these days when Belial's strong
Scorch us with thy flaming song !

Thee, oh fighter for decrees
That gave the common people ease,
Who against lords and loyalties
Upheld the learn'd laws penalties,
We ask who are but common men
Uphold us with thy scholard pen.

Yea ! To us all whose bodies are bound
To till with sweat another's ground,
As a master, teach that litany,
" Deliver us from the tyranny
Of all false knaves that filch by stealth
From the common men their commonwealth !"

32. TO MY LADY'S DELICATE EAR.

Through all my heart's imagining
I have sought for you a perfect thing.
I have sought and thought and planned and
    wrought,
That you should find no word amiss
In sense or sound or harmonies;
But in a settled, sequent string
These lines with melody should sing,
And every verse should rhyme and ring
Upon your ear, a perfect thing.

www.ingramcontent.com/pod-product-compliance
Lightning Source LLC
Chambersburg PA
CBHW071310030720
47593CB00003B/1284